Capri
Capri

CENTRO STAMPA EDITORIALE
plurigraf
PERSEUS

Indice
Index

L'isola di Capri

The island of Capri

The island of Capri, a geographical prolongation of the Sorrento Peninsula, closes the Bay of Naples to the south, just as the island of Ischia, to the north, gave a foretaste of the beauties of this part of Italy.

Thus Capri embraces the marvels of this stretch of coast and faces the no less picturesque landscape of the Bay of Salerno.
It is a small island, covering barely 10 Kilometres, and is roughly quadrangular in shape.
One is immediately struck by the cliffs rising sheer out of the sea, the luxurious vegetation covering most of the island, and the dazzling white houses scattered among the green.
The little town of Capri is the main centre.
To the west stands Anacapri, on a high plateau on the slopes of Monte Solaro.
Most of the inhabitants live in these two places.
Most of the fishermen's families live at Marina Grande, which is also the island's main port, while Marina Piccola, situated on the South coast, is a very popular little resort in a marvellous position.
Naturally, tourism is the main business of the island's inhabitants, but some of the people are engaged in fishing and cultivating olive groves and vine yards.
The island's flora and fauna (especially as regards fish), are particularly interesting and varied.
The flora above all, thanks to the large number of species present, is a valuable asset to the island and one of its many beauties.
To list all the beauties that have made Capri world famous, would only mean making a mere enumeration without actually capturing its spirit.
Capri is a jewel box full of gems, and this is principally thanks to Nature.
The Blue Grotto, the Faraglioni, the Natural Arch, the countless other grottoes scattered along its coast and the steep cliffs falling sheer into the sea, are only a few of its best known features.
In addition, there are the magnificent views, the picturesque depths with crystal clear wates, the numerous parks and public gardens, the characteristic architecture of the houses, and the local colour that can be noted in the buildings and the handicraft products.
Nor should one overlook the interesting remains of the Roman era, such as those of the splendid Villa Jovis, or Villa Damecuta, and the beautiful Villa San Michele dating from the early years of this century.
Capri has been rightly called the Pearl of the Sea: to know it means to rediscover the creative force of Nature and the sense of its beauty.

P
SNA 1152
NESSUNO

CARMEN

Marina Grande

Marina Grande

Marina Grande is the ancient port of Capri and the only important landing place, owing to the island, particular morphology with cliffs falling sheer to the sea all along its coastline.

The other landing place (though not the main one) is situated on the south coast of the island, where the attractive little resort of Marina Piccola lies. Marina Grande is well equipped to accommodate private yachts and the countless regular services which bring thousands upon thousands of tourists here every year from the various harbours of the Bay of Naples. The village of Marina Grande extends along the Bay of Capri, with its row of typical and attractive fishermen's cottages, huddling one against the other, almost forming a single mass and distinguishable only by their bright, varied colours. From Marina Grande a road leads to the little town of Capri and other places on the island, and there is also a funicular that starts here and goes straight up to Capri. There is a regular boats service from the port to the Blue Grotto. Let us take a last look at the island as a whole before going up to Capri and Anacapri. From the harbour of Marina Grande the two high rocky spurs can be seen rising up, above which there are two small plateaus. To the west, in the line of Monte Solaro, stands

Prewious pages: View of Marina Grande.

The funicular railway.

Anacapri, to the east Monte Tiberio. Capri lies in the little valley between the two peaks, nestling on the slopes of Monte Tiberio. Dense vegetation covers all the lower part of the island, while higher up the rock rises steep and bare; at other points it falls sheer to the sea, creating inlets, grottoes and most picturesque corners.

View of Marina Grande.

The island has a good public transport service; in fact, during certain periods of the year residents are prohibited from using their cars in order to reduce traffic, which gets very congested in the high season. The flow of tourists is so great that for some years now there has been talk of imposing a limit on entry. One can move around quite easily by using public transport – buses or taxis - although the most impressive trip is surely that by funicular railway. From Marina Grande, one can take the funicular railway to the centre of Capri; this delightful and unusual means of transport, gives one the opportunity of admiring some enchanting scenery, in fact, the route climbs up the fertile, cultivated slopes where houses appear to cling to the rocks.

Capri

Capri

The road, which starts from Marina Grande, leads up to the centre of Capri in a series of steep twists and turns.

Before venturing into the characteristic narrow lanes of the little town, the visitor's gaze can roam over Marina Grande beneath and the coast of Sorrento in the distance. It is a truly breath-taking view, but still finer ones await us. The inhabitants call this Belvedere "the little balcony", for this is what it looks like. It is situated in the open space at the terminus of the funicular railway.

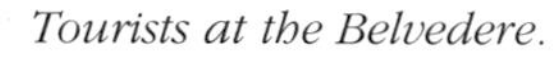

Tourists at the Belvedere.

One side of the Piazzetta is taken up by the Church of Santo Stefano. In front of it there is a wide flight of steps, where tourists are wont to sit, to rest and enjoy the busy life of the Piazzetta and the mild air of the island.

The church, a local version of the baroque style, stands on the site of the ancient cathedral.

It was rebuilt several times and contains valuable works of art, of which the fine polychrome marble floor deserves particular mention.

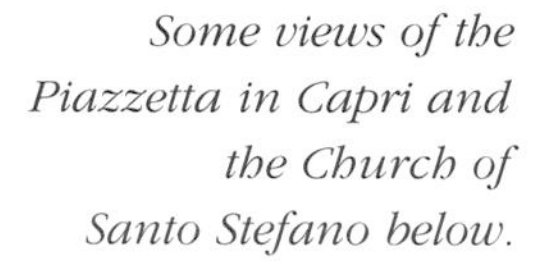

Some views of the Piazzetta in Capri and the Church of Santo Stefano below.

Capri: in giro per la città

Capri: touring the town

We leave the square now and make our way into the narrow streets of the town: wandering down the Via dei Fornai, Via Botteghe, Via Camerelle, Via Longano (where a plaque records that Maxim Gorky lived here, and here entertained Lenin when the latter fled into exile). Via Posterula, Via Madre Serafina, and into the elegant Via Vittorio Emanuele, where we find further breathtaking views and curious corners.

Brightly-coloured maiolica earthenware, a typical handicraft of the island.

Typical Capri sandals, also made to measure.

Some views of Via delle Camerelle.

The bright colours of the boutiques and souvenir stalls, overflowing with goods, add a note of vitality to the natural tones of the island, pleasing the eye of the beholder. These are not sights one easily forgets: the medieval maze of the town, the white-washed homes, the balconies brimming with blooms, the vistas of mountain and sea. Despite the chatter going on around one, despite the numbers of people that throng these streets, one is always aware of a deep silence and peace within. Perhaps because everything is so clean and pure, so bright and cheery, so sun-filled and warm. The Church of Sant'Anna (St Anne) is also worth a visit in Capri. This simple structure was built in the 12th century and is swallowed up among the houses in the medieval quarter. A pretty bell-tower rises from the facade. Then there is the Church of San Salvatore (Our Saviour) going back to the 17th century, and the Convent which was founded by Sister Serafina of God.

La Certosa di San Giacomo

The Monastery of St. James

Partially restored, the monumental construction includes the church and convent, which enclose a small 14th century cloister dominated by the baroque clocktower and the late 16th century cloister.

Erected in 1371-74 by Count Giacomo Arcucci, feudal lord of the island, the charterhouse of S. Giacomo remains, despite numerous reconstructions, the most important example of Capri architecture which, slowly maturing midst the ruins of Roman villas, found in the oldest churches and the monumental Certosa its truest creations thanks to local craftsmen faithful to the Roman tradition.
The domed roofs of the house and churches provide a harmonious and rational harmony with nature.
Castles, churches and houses weave together with the ruins of the Roman villas a modulated consonance of volumes, forms and colours in the Capri countryside.
Thus from the imperial villa on Mount Tiberius to the majestic charterhouse between the heights of Tuoro and Castiglione opposite the Faraglioni, the passage from the imperial hermitage to the monastic hermitage seems obvious and natural.
The Certosa was not only the ideal place for the ascetic life of the monks but also an economic force on the island, with possessions extending here and there and even around Naples.
Devastated by pirates during the 16th century, the charterhouse was restored by the monks who erected a defensive tower, which collapsed in 1808.
Following disagreements between the regular clergy, and the secular clergy the charter-

house was suppressed in 1807 by Giuseppe Bonaparte and, thereafter, had various uses.
The large cloister is surrounded by a pillared portico around which are grouped the cells, dispensary, capitulary, garden and other rooms.
To the right on the cliff edge is the Prior's quarters isolated from the rest of the convent and probably constructed in the 16th century.
Of considerable interest is the Church which has an ogival portal decorated with bas-relief figures of St. Bruno and St. Giacomo and a 13th century fresco. The inside has only one nave and the vault and cross- vault is characteristic in Capri architecture.

THE CERTOSA MUSEUM

Standing near the church is the Certosa Museum displaying a few statues recovered from the seabed of Grotta Azzurra, which are corroded by the seawater. According to some, these statues go to prove that at the time of Emperors Augustus and Tiberius the grotto was a nymphaea, which false legends later linked to the equally legendary Tiberian horrors, while remains of building work, now submerged, go to show the notable drop in level of the Grotta Azzurra from Roman times to the present day. Other works worth mentioning are the 17th and 18th century paintings and a collection of works by the German artist Karl Wilhelm Diefenbach, who lived in Capri from the year 1900 until his death in 1913.

Il Parco di Augusto ed i Faraglioni

The Park of Augustus and the Faraglioni

The Gardens of Augustus are along the road that leads to the Certosa di San Giacomo and are not far from the town of Capri.

This is one of the most picturesque places of Capri; it is a public garden with a wealth of various plants, criss-crossed by paths, lanes and steps leading to the various view-points, from which one can see the southern part of island, the Marina Piccola below, and most of all, the famous Faraglioni, emerging like little rocky islands from the deep blue water.

Via Krupp.

View of the Giardini di Augusto (Park of Augustus).

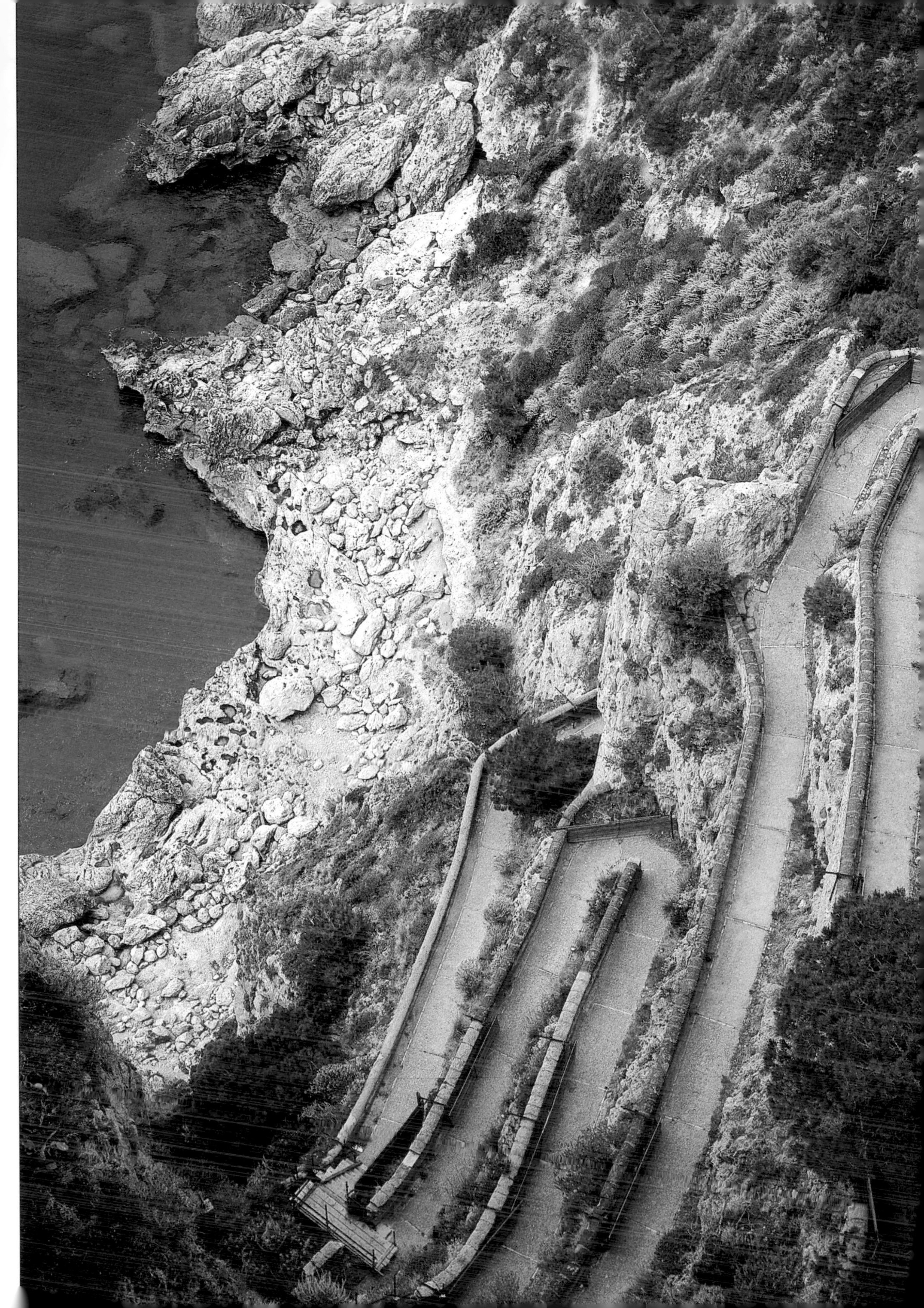

Tutti i colori del mare

All the colours of the sea

The beauties of Capri are not just limited to what can be found on the land, for the underwater landscapes too are full of life and colour.

In the island there are many places where it is possible to go sub-acqua diving, or try the more specialist snorkelling, a trip in the sea water, equipped with mask, fins and oxygen.
The discovery of this underwater world is a marvel, with the fascinating play of light which is offered by the many rocky caves and cavities.

Marina Piccola

Marina Piccola

This is the other landing place (after Marina Grande) of which the island can boast.

Well equipped, and favoured by the special advantages of its surroundings, it is one of the most popular and sought-after holiday resorts, a refined and luxurious place for sea bathing.

Bathing resort.

VILLA MALAPARTE

The fascination of Capri also struck the writer Curzio Malaparte (whose real name was Kurt Sukert, born in Prato in 1898 and died in Rome in 1957). After a brief stay on the island he fell in love with it and decided to build himself a villa there. Today, Villa Malaparte is considered a masterpiece of italian Rationalism.

Arco Naturale

The Natural Arch

The particular kind of rock on the island (limestone) has given rise to some fantastic shapes.

External agents, such as wind and rain, operating for centuries on these rocky cliffs, have transformed the appearance of the rock faces, creating fantastic and sometimes daring shapes, like, for instance, the so-called Natural Arch.
There is also an interesting natural cave, the Grotta di Matromania, used by the ancient Romans as a place of worship of Cybele (interesting remains of mosaic decorations and masonry are found here).

I piaceri della tavola

The Pleasures of Eating

On par with the tourist itinerary is the gastronomic one, and equally a pleasure, dotted with small and large eating places, which offer true masterpieces of cuisine.

Capri-style cooking is a perfect combination of both produce from land and sea. Plain, simple cooking which respects the natural flavours of the ingredients.

Some of the most famous products the land has to offer are the juicy lemons, which, apart from delicious jams, are also used in the preparation of "Limoncello", an after-dinner liqueur of ancient homely origin. Apart from the juicy, highly-scented lemons, we can enjoy sweet small tomatoes called "SPUNZILLI", which are hung up and preserved, and tasty mature and fresh cheeses such as scamorza, caciotta, a variety of mozzarellas and caciocavallo.

Some typical first courses include SCIALATIELLI (durum wheat fettuccine or ribbon-pasta without egg), VERMICELLI and CAVATIELLI (similar to orecchiette pasta, small pasta discs), and CANNARUCCIELLI (long fettuccine pasta) mixed with seafood sauce, hen-clam sauce, spunzilli sauce (dried tomatoes), capers, olives and anchovies. One can easily imagine what an extraordinary variety of fish the sea has to offer: bass, dory, "pezzogne" and "sarago" (two Mediterranean fish). The most common method of cooking these fish is the "acqua pazza" (mad water) recipe, which consists of a mixture of seawater, oil, parsley and dried toma-

A typical cake.

LIMONCELLO

<u>Ingredients</u>: 6 lemons (organic), 1/2 litre alcohol, 1/2 litre water, 1/2 kg sugar.

<u>Preparation</u>: Bring to the boil half a litre of water, allow it to cool, then add the lemon rinds, half a litre of alcohol and half a kilo of sugar. Leave the mixture to stand for 15 days, then filter and serve cold.

toes. This place is a food-lover's paradise: the confectioner's shop-windows are abundant in delicacies ranging from the simple Capri cake to lemon cream-filled profiteroles.

Pezzogne fish in "Acqua Pazza".

TAGLIOLINI ALLO SCOGLIO

(Thin tagliatelle or ribbon-pasta with a seafood sauce). Ingredients: (Serves 4) 320 g tagliolini pasta, 250 g cockles, 250 g mussels, 250 g hen-clams, 1 pepper, 1 hot dried chilli, 8 "spunzilli" (dried tomatoes), a sprig of parsley, 2 cloves of garlic, 6 tablespoons of extra virgin olive oil, salt and white pepper. Preparation: Wash the mollusc shells under running water, place the hen-clams and cockles in abundant salted water and leave to purge for 3 hours, after which rinse and scrub the mussels well. Then place them all in a large pan, add 2 tablespoons of oil, a sprig of parsley, pepper and a clove of garlic. Cover the pan and cook on a high flame till they open up. Remove the molluscs and filter the cooking liquid. First remove the skins from the dried tomatoes, then cut them into pieces. Clean the pepper, de-seed and chop into small pieces. Fry it for about 5 minutes in a pan with the rest of the oil, chilli and remainder of the garlic. Add the chopped tomatoes and cook for 10-15 minutes, adding the cooking liquid used for the shells. Boil the tagliolini pasta for just 2 minutes, drain and mix it with part of the prepared sauce. Place the pasta on foil sheets, pour over the remaining sauce and the shells, sprinkle over the chopped parsley, close the foil parcels and cook in a pre-heated oven, at 200°, for 5-6 minutes, after which remove the foil parcels and serve.

Villa Jovis

Villa Jovis

Villa Jovis, the largest and best conserved of the island's imperial villas, unites historical interest and the singular beauty of the site.

Inhabited since prehistoric times, as shown by weapons and implements found, it was part of the Greek colonies first and later Roman, and then in 29 AD Capri passed from its solitary existence as a small island to the centre of Imperial Roman life. It was in that year that Ottaviano, (not yet Augustus) while sailing towards Naples, was attracted by the soaring cliffs and the gigantic peaks of the Faraglioni.
He landed at Capri and so delightful was his stay that he did not hesitate to withdraw the island from Naple's domain and make it part of the growing principality. Ottaviano, frequently stayed in Capri almost until his death in 14 AD and after his death Tiberius made Capri an imperial residence. However, while Augustus serenely loved Capri, Tiberius, the misanthopist, old was a splendid and jealous lover; from this morbid love and his bitter delight in exile and solitude comes the myth of Tiberius, a legend which, even

The ruins of Villa Jovis.

View of Marina Grande from Villa Jovis.

today, gives life to the deserted ruins of the palazzi and Roman villas of Capri.

Mythical, too, is the number of 12 villas which, according to Tacito, the emperor had built on the island, corrisponding in number to the twelve divinities of Olympus.

Unfortunately, owing to rearrangements made through the centuries, it is no longer possible to control the number of the villas and their sites.

Only three have been verified and, indeed, excel for their grandiose structure and the vast area they cover: one on the Damecuta Plain, a second, known as Palazzo on the Sea, with a descent leading to the Tiberius Baths and, finally, the third, Villa Jovis, which crowns

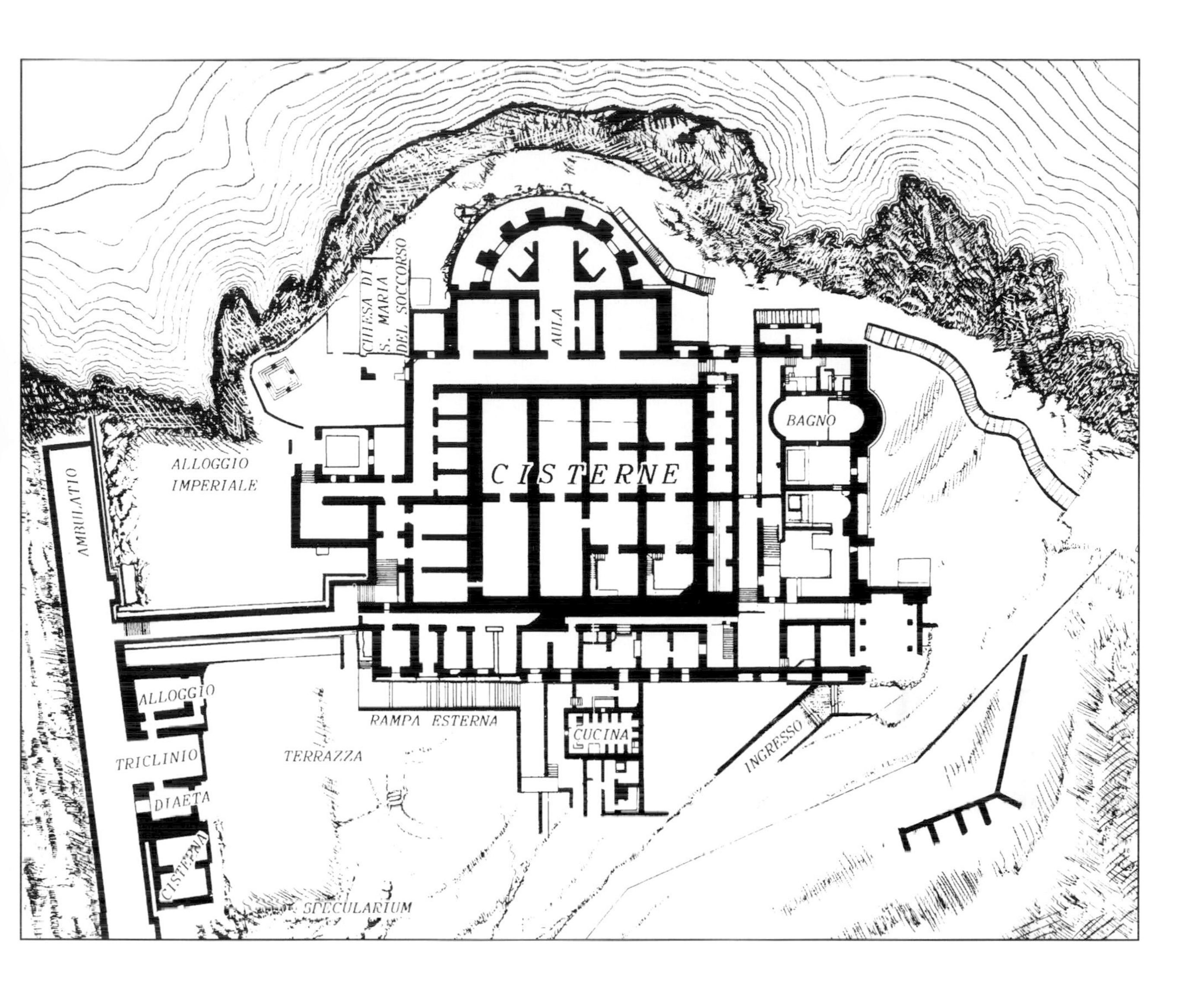

the eastern headland of the island where Jupiter and his earthly pontiff Tiberius could surround themselves with brilliant awesome, splendour.
Near the entrance to the excavations is the so-called Tiberius Jump, a frightening, rocky precipice 297 metres above the sea, from where, according to tradition Tiberius forced his victims to leap.
Villa Jovis, was the favourite residence of Tiberius who stayed on the island for the last ten years of his life (26-37 AD), with a small following, and administered the Empire from here. This was the most splendid period in the ancient history of Capri despite the fame of Tiberius' perversity.
In any case, the assertion by some that after Tiberius' death the Senate ordered all his villas on Capri to be demolished is merely a legend. The island, infact, continued to be frequented by successive emperors and Roman aristocrats and the important garrison established in Tiberius'time to protect him remained.
Remembered by both Svetonio and Plinius, the Villa covers the summit of Mount Tiberius with an area of 7000 square metres. With woods, gardens and nympheae the area covered must have been greater still. The building, with floors and terraces connected by stairways, extends from Torre del Faro, probably of the Tiberian era, to the summit of the promontory. The various quarters are centred around a square area, which has four cisterns carved in the rock to collect rain water.
To the worth is a large panoramic terrace, probably the most grandiose part of the original structure.
Looted during the first excavations in Burbon times, stripped of its marble floors and tampered with in the course of the centuries, the villa was first explored in 1827. Only in 1932 and 1935 A. Maiuri completed the excavations, which brought this splendid villa fully to light a villa of the first half of the Empire.

Grotta Azzurra

Blue Grotto

Celebrated as one of the wonders of our coast, the grotto was known to the ancients as has been shown from the Roman remains found both inside and outside the groto.

A high rocky spur which extends in a sea of blue, cliffs to which cling trees twisted by the wind into the strangest forms, tiny roads with white walls which lead to little houses wither still, a square crowded night and day with the life which elsewhere seems hidden, modern hotels, shops, the crowd with famous names, strangely dressed figures and simple folk. Capri is this and more, few places in Italy have so many faces so different and varied grouped together in such a small space as Capri.

The island owes its worldwide fame to the splendid natural beauty, the ancient wyths and legends, the fascinating remains of imperial villas, the characteristic domes of the houses and churches but most of all to the

famous marine cathedral that is the Blue Grotto.
This ancient cave in the northern coast of the island, made larger by landslides and lowered by the effect of bradysism so as to be partially under sea level owes its fame to particular its geological conditions. The tiny entrance only two meters wide and one metre high means that the grotto receives light which has passed underwater. This light freed from the water colours the walls, roof and stalactites an intense blue.
The light makes the water opalescent and anything submerged in the water appears silver. Tiberius probably transformed the grotto into a nymphea, a sort of temple dedicated to marine gods.
It was easily reached from Villa di Gradola the ruins of which are above the grotto. In time the existence of the grotto as forgotten even though the inhabitants of Capri knew of it before Angelo Ferraro's visit on 16th May 1822 and indeed visited the grotto before the apparent discovery by the poet Augusto Kopish of Breslavia and his friends on 17th August 1826. In any case it was at this time that the grotto made its official entrance in the list of natural wonders of Capri and began with its magic colour to increase the fame of Capri.
Thus the myth of the sirens has returned to where it was born, in the sea in the recesses of a magic cliff which men can enter through a narrow fissure and find the magic spectacle of the grotto. Once inside looking down in the crystal water to the tiny pebbles at the bottom or looking around at the blue rock wrapped in an enchanted light it is possible to discover the secret fascination that is Capri.

The road that led from Marina Grande to Capri, now goes up to the other little town on the island, Anacapri. All the way, the road cut into the rock climbs up steeply and one has a continuous succession of marvellous views: the eye ranges not only over Capri and Marina Grande, but embraces in the distance the coastline of Sorrento. At the top, from the parapet at a height of some 300 metres above sea level, we are met by the extraordinary sight of the sheer wall of rock plunging down into the sea. It is a truly impressive sight.

The Blue Grotto.

Anacapri

Anacapri is the second town on the island after Capri. It stands on the slopes of Monte Solaro, 275 metres above sea level, a level piece of ground, which is particularly rich in natural and cultivated vegetation.

The rocks and the luxuriant greenery make it an attractive place, popular with those visitors who seek a quiet and restful holiday on the island. Anacapri is a high class holiday centre which attracts crowds of visitors every year, thanks aso to the quality and efficiency of the accommodation it offers.
There are many shops and popular boutiques, and hee too,

Panorama of Anacapri.

View from the terrace of Hotel Cesare Augusto.

one finds the characteristic stalls in a row all along the edge of the road, striking a homely note among the luxurious hotels, restaurants and cafes.
Anacapri is also the best starling point for excursions to Monte Solaro, and also for visiting the famous Villa San Michele, the Imperial Roman Villa and the Blue Grotto.
Via Orlandi and the Piazza della Vittoria form the centre of Anacapri.

The parish church of Santa Sofia and the Caprile quarter around the little square of the same name, are also worth a visit. Anacapri is the starting place for the excursion to Monte Solaro (589 metres), an excursion the tourist should not miss if he wishes to know the whole of Capri, and get a complete view

The Church of Santa Sofia.

The chair-lift to Monte Solaro.

of the island from the highest point.
The top can be reached on foot by way of Via San Michele (only recommended by good walkers), or by the chair-lift, which has its Lower Station in Piazza della Vittoria at Anacapri.
The chair-lift glides over woods and clearings, reaching the top of the mountain in about 15 minutes.
Here we are 589 metres above sea level; the island is stretched out below. We can recognise its shape and its various points, ranging with the eye over the manifold beauties of this rock which rises from the sea: all around us lies this little world where luxuriant nature reigns supreme. Near the summits is the 14th century Sanctuary of Santa Maria di Cetrella.

Panorama from Monte Solaro.

Majestic scenery viewed from Monte Solaro.

La Scala Fenicia
The Phoenician Steps

In ancient times, and up to the end of the last century, this was the only way one could reach the town.

The Swedish doctor, Axel Munthe, who visited the island and chose to build his home in Anacapri, used this stairway, with the knowledge that he was following in the footsteps of generations of islanders before him. It is undoubtedly possessed of a special fascination which increases in relation to its history: it represents a corner of the past, a rare and exceptional relic of the ancient colonizers of this land. To climb these stairs means to have some strange share in that far-off time, to retrace step by step, the slow yet persistent path of man's conquests.

Il Faro di Punta Carena
The lighthouse at Punta Carena

The lighthouse, a large red building, stands on the Carena Point on the extreme south-west of the island.

Inspite of roads and increasing traffic, Capri is one of the few places left where old mule tracks and paths allow visitors to enjoy on foot the natural beauty of the is" land'. Anybody who thinks he can get to know the island visiting it in a car is illuding himself. The tourist should visit the island on foot to appreciate it in full, a lit. tle like the drinker who sips his wine so as to enjoy the flavour a perfume, in this way the visitor will discover the most fascinating if less obvious aspects of this island. Capri today is one of the best equipped intenational tourist resorts.

A far cry from the time when an adventurous boat trip from Naples ended with simple homely hospitality of the locals as was the case for the first 18th century travellers who made Capri famous all over Europe.
Since then the tourist facilities have developed into a thriving modern industry with countless hotels sporting and bathing facilities and nightclubs.
Communications with Naples are now easy and comfortable with frequent boat trips or hydrofoils which bring the numcrous tourists from the mainland to Capri.

Le grotte di Capri
The Grottos of Capri

One of the most enchanting and extraordinary aspects of Capri is the natural architecture of the coast with its variety of form and colour and the numerous grottos at sea level with their fabulous phosphorescent light.

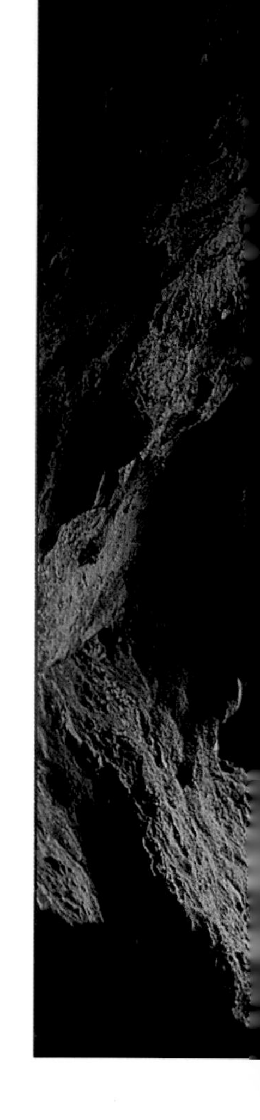

The sea has modelled and erroded these bizare caverns, roars in the dark recesses, laps against the encrusted walls and filters the blue light. Each and every grotto has a particular characteristic for which it is famous: The Green Grotto for example (once called the Turk's Grotto) has water of a brilliant emerald green. The Marvellous Grotto owes it name to the marvellous stalagmites.

The Saints Grotto.

The Arsenal Grotto is of particular interest because it was mistakenly believed to have been a naval shipyard but was in reality a roman nymphaea as shown by the podium and coloured marbles found.

The Matromania Grotto

The Green Grotto.

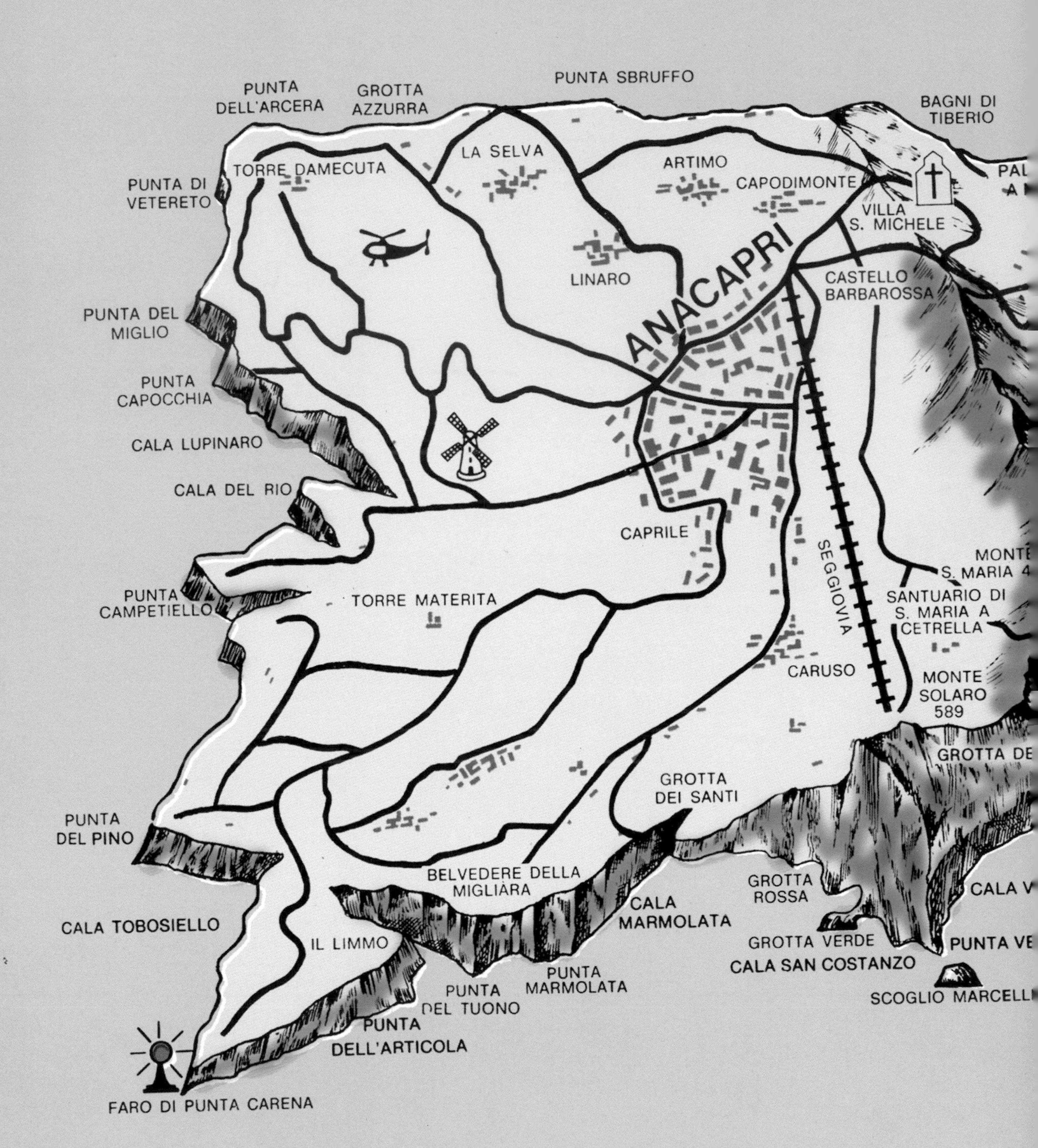
PUNTA SBRUFFO
PUNTA DELL'ARCERA
GROTTA AZZURRA
BAGNI DI TIBERIO
TORRE DAMECUTA
LA SELVA
ARTIMO
CAPODIMONTE
PUNTA DI VETERETO
VILLA S. MICHELE
ANACAPRI
LINARO
CASTELLO BARBAROSSA
PUNTA DEL MIGLIO
PUNTA CAPOCCHIA
CALA LUPINARO
CALA DEL RIO
CAPRILE
SEGGIOVIA
PUNTA CAMPETIELLO
TORRE MATERITA
SANTUARIO DI S. MARIA A CETRELLA
CARUSO
MONTE SOLARO 589
GROTTA DEI SANTI
PUNTA DEL PINO
BELVEDERE DELLA MIGLIARA
GROTTA ROSSA
CALA MARMOLATA
CALA TOBOSIELLO
IL LIMMO
GROTTA VERDE
CALA SAN COSTANZO
PUNTA MARMOLATA
PUNTA DEL TUONO
PUNTA DELL'ARTICOLA
FARO DI PUNTA CARENA

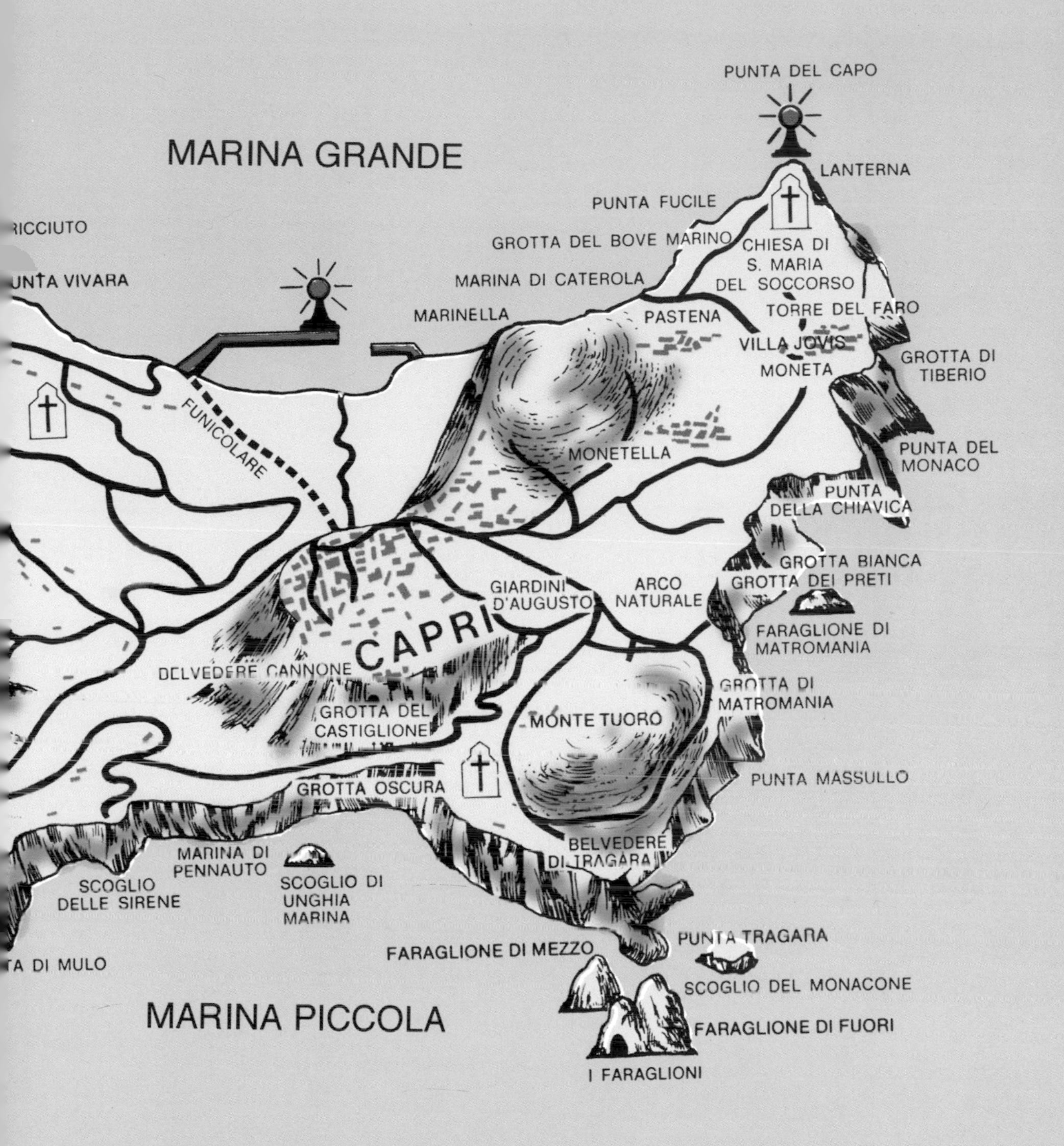
MARINA GRANDE
PUNTA DEL CAPO
LANTERNA
PUNTA FUCILE
GROTTA DEL BOVE MARINO
CHIESA DI
S. MARIA
DEL SOCCORSO
MARINA DI CATEROLA
TORRE DEL FARO
PASTENA
MARINELLA
VILLA JOVIS
MONETA
GROTTA DI
TIBERIO
FUNICOLARE
MONETELLA
PUNTA DEL
MONACO
PUNTA
DELLA CHIAVICA
GROTTA BIANCA
GROTTA DEI PRETI
GIARDINI
D'AUGUSTO
ARCO
NATURALE
CAPRI
FARAGLIONE DI
MATROMANIA
BELVEDERE CANNONE
GROTTA DI
MATROMANIA
GROTTA DEL
CASTIGLIONE
MONTE TUORO
PUNTA MASSULLO
GROTTA OSCURA
BELVEDERE
DI TRAGARA
MARINA DI
PENNAUTO
SCOGLIO
DELLE SIRENE
SCOGLIO DI
UNGHIA
MARINA
PUNTA TRAGARA
FARAGLIONE DI MEZZO
SCOGLIO DEL MONACONE
FARAGLIONE DI FUORI
I FARAGLIONI
MARINA PICCOLA

Text: Loretta Santini

Revision: Anna Caprespa

Photos: Archivio Plurigraf - Jab Capri - Atlantide - Sie

Acknowledgements: Jab Capri - Alberino Gennarino - Oasi Monte Barbarossa - Azienda Autonoma di cura soggiorno e turismo, isola di Capri - Ente per il turismo, regione Campania

Published and printed by Centro Stampa Editoriale, Sesto Fiorentino, (Fi).